If any of these poems bring forth life or shed light in your life it will have served its purpose. Thanks for your purchase and many blessings to you and yours.

Marcelto Cooks

Acknowledgments

If it had not been for His grace and mercy I would not be where I am or who I am….and the best is yet to come.

I thank God for the places he has brought me from and through. I am thankful for those who thought they were suppressing me but were ultimately part of God's perfect plan for my life.

To my mothers, my brothers, and my sisters, thank you for your love and support.

To my sons and daughters, I am thankful for your individual, unique personalities. Know that I am always praying for your safety, strength, and growth in the Lord.

To my two grans, I am thankful for your perfect smiles which are an inspiration. I pray that you will grow into the people that God has created you to be.

To my beautiful wife, my Isay, I love you. For a man who is filled with words, there are none that fully express the love and gratitude that I have for you. Thank you for being able to see things in me that I couldn't always see for myself.

My Hands, His Words

Marcelto L. Cooks was born and raised in Columbus, Georgia. The Peabody housing projects was one of the many places this second born child of Judy Cooks called home. As a child Marcelto was passionate about nearly every subject. Early on he began to express himself through drawing. This was the beginning of the artistic ability that he would later learn to express through words. Drawing calmed Marcelto and became his means of escape from all the things around him. Things that he later learned to express through rhythmic words placed uniquely together to form his poetry. At the age of nine his love of drawing would come to share time with something else. Rap Music. Rap was introduced to him through the eyes and mind of his older brother, Alfonte Cooks. Marcelto fell in love with the freedom of expression. The word play consumed him, drawing him into the giant world of hip-hop. He ate, sweat, and bled rap music. He testified to its wonders and displayed its pain. Marcelto was the raw that was rap music in its roughest, truest light. To be able to express him self through rap was exactly what he needed at the time. It released him and helped him to survive all the pitfalls of life. His love for rap took him to the door of poetry. He developed a natural passion for poetry, the art he was predestined to partake of and contribute to. Marcelto's means before poetry prepared him for it. Through this art he escaped from death and the world it existed in. This Christian man's words are filled with the love that pain brought. They are filled with life and the lessons it has taught; its joys and pains, its love and hates. Marcelto now brings to all who enjoy, the simple yet beautiful enigma called poetry.

The Good, the Bad, and the Ugly; the battle of the Spirit and the Flesh	7
Just Tired	8
Who…. What	9
over	10
Fear Not	11
A Voice	12
I Was Once	13
411	14
Do You Take	15
He was there for me	16
The Gladiator	17
Gather	19
THE JUNGLE	20
Got To Know Life	22
My Brothers	23
The Perfect Poem	24
I am here	27
Mind your steps	28
Burn	30
Soul of an old song	32
One and the Same	33
I Can	35
Know your fight	37
They Win	38
Mercy Mercy	39
It wasn't	41
Discontent	42
Hello Day Break	44
Tomorrows Death	46
Refuge	47

Changing Spots	48
Here	49
Wake me please	50
XXXXXXXX	52
Find your way	53
4x4	54
(Live What) My Life or Yours	55
You can not define me	56
Page 3 my diary	58
You owe	59
Brick yard	60
Keep Walking	63
I've Got a Man	64
Values	66
Alone	68
What good is a poem	70
My giant	73
War inside me	75
The Rules Are	76
Pick it Up	78
Peace	82

The Good, the Bad, and the Ugly; the battle of the Spirit and the Flesh

I'm happy, but I'm sad,
I'm strong, but I'm weak,
I'm scared, but I'm brave,
I'm shallow, but I'm deep,
I'm mean, but I'm nice,
I can see, but I'm blind,
I'm a follower, but I'm a leader,
I'm wrong, but I'm right,
I'm dead at times, but at other times
I'm so full of life,
I'm sarcastic, but I'm serious,
I'm full of joy, but I'm also full of pain,
Sometimes I enjoy the sunshine,
At other times I enjoy the rain,
I'm calm natured, but I'm unruly,
I've hated and I've loved,
I've seen and I've touched,
I've had so little,
But then again, I've had so very much,
I'm empty, but I'm full,
I'm soft, but I'm tough,
I've been asleep and I've been awake,
I've been smooth and I've been rough,
I'm all these things at times,
But there is one thing
I always was and always will be,
A child of God,
Despite the good, the bad, and the ugly.

Just Tired

Tired of the games
The liars
The procrastinators
The haters
So called keep it reala's
and all the rest of the fakers

The phony
The fraudulent
The cheaters
and all of the weak

The unfocused fronting counterfeiters
that run these streets

The petty
The immoral
The ignorant idolizing
Indecent ingrates
The incorrigible
The disrespectful

Parasites that make
Indecisive unconscious decisions to take
the moral and turn it from the truth to fake

I've run a lot of roads
but I now know which road to take

Who.... What

To be or not to be was never
the question for me;

A pawn in the game,
but I was always destined to be;

Not a queen but a king,
yes I will change the game;

Come what may, know that things
won't stay the same;

I am
what I am
and who I am
for good reason.

over

i sit here in this hole
contemplating time
a life with a wife
who was probably never mine

a journey began at whatever point
we as mature adults started
and it ends where we left
one another broken hearted

when we wrong each other
in so many ways
and through thought
patience
and endurance
i tried to save

i am only a man
and can do nothing
with what I have no control over

at first i hurt and felt like life was over
but through God and strength i knew better

i now understand that what God does not
want will not last

Fear Not

The stars in the sky aren't afraid to shine,

The minutes in an hour aren't afraid of time,

The fish in the sea aren't afraid to drown,

The color rainbow isn't afraid of brown,

The cells in the body aren't afraid of blood,

The two beautiful doves aren't afraid of love,

The pages of the book aren't afraid to turn,

The fire once lit isn't afraid to burn,

The ice in the North Pole isn't
afraid of the cold,

The little tree in the forest will not
be afraid to grow,

The play on Broadway isn't afraid to show,

The truth is something I'm not afraid to know,

Fear not my people it is time to grow,

Gods got us" (July 5 2003)

A Voice

Pain, anguish, and agony are the legs, on which I stand;

And I made it that way, WHY? You wouldn't understand.

In this land, this land our forefathers built with their bare hands;

This land where the civil aren't civilized and a baby can kill a full-grown man.

We are not doing our part; it's not that we aren't smart; we've just lost our heart;

That ability to take a child and raise them to be just, not raise them to be us,

but to be a voice............

I Was Once

The fiery flower that bloomed alone in the depth of winter,

The fearful cries of the faceless repented who dare go where it says Do Not Enter.

Look and you'll find the shame-filled sinner (I Was Once).

Open the book, then read all the pages,

Criticize the others that were also faced with the same inequality that had placed us where we all were so very hopeless,

Judge not for fear of judgment,

One who didn't fear God, but feared the government (I Was Once).

Imprisoned by the four walls of hatred, came out the closet only to hide in the basement.

This confusion was merely displacement from what we all were afraid of facing.

These words are short, but to the point, a man of the world (I Was Once).

411

If talking about someone else today is
important for you to do,
Then maybe I am not the one for
you to be talking to,
For if you want to talk lets talk
but we will talk about me and you,
For you and I are ear to ear,
you hear me and I hear you,
The confusion state of he say she say can't
stand in our way,
For you speak your truth and I'll speak my
truth this way we can honestly say,
You told me and I told you and john doe had
nothing to say,
For you said your part and I said mine,
john doe had nothing to say,
We're one on one you and I so ask about me
and I'll ask about you,
Don't tell me what john said about doe
because that does not concern you,
If we're going to help john lets help john,
there is no need to talk ,
I don't need to know johns business to help
him I will merely walk the walk,
Don't be upset….. ok I'll talk to you later since
our conversation is done,
You and I can only speak on you and I and
that's the 411.

Do You Take

WIVES LEARN YOUR HUSBANDS,
HUSBANDS LEARN YOUR WIVES

For you need to understand you no
longer live separate lives,

What God has joined together let
no man put asunder,

The union of man and woman is one
of God's greatest wonders,

For wives understand that there is but
one that comes before your mate,

Husbands know that the same applies to you,
for there are some things that can't be
replaced.

He was there for me

Talk that big talk, call me crazy if you want,
you can even keep tryin to make
me change my faith;
keep tryin to feed me that stuff about never
seeing **his** face. Keep tryin to make me follow
you and all that you believe;
but you'll never know the love I have
for **him** because **he** was there for me.
Where were you when I slept so many
nights outside in the cold?
Where were you, I ask, when I needed
someone to know…..
to know all that I went through when I was
hungry and feeling weak?
You weren't there to help me
overcome my fears
when I was scared and felt alone;
when I was blind and lost in the world **he**
helped me to find my way home.
He's the one, who taught this man to
cry to bring those things out of me,
though I was brainwashed by the streets,
he's the one who set me free.
So say what you must and say what you
will but one day you'll see,
no matter what men think,
he was there for me.

The Gladiator

The ground rumbled and the skies crackled as the master sent out his greatest gladiator to do battle with every man and beast.

He was as graceful as he was masterful and he wielded a sword from the heavens.

As he entered the arena to do battle, his enemies would fall to his feet and plead for him to let them flea without the penalty of being scorned and defeated.

To speak of this gladiator and his undying will to do what ever his master asked of him inspired me to be as brave as he. I can only hope to walk as he walked and be as merciful and loving as he, for as he went to do battle he did not weep nor did he complain.

He just fell in and did as he was instructed, fighting every battle with as much passion as the first. This brave warrior was and still is the mightiest gladiator the world as ever known.

The funny thing is he killed so many only to save them and in doing this he only drew blood once, his own. Gladiator, I must call you my lord, for he did and still does battle for us so that we may be saved.

One came to do battle with the whole world that we all may be saved. He is the Gladiator, the Messiah, the Christ, and our Lord Jesus.

Gather

Let us gather
Let us gather under what we can feel but not touch
What we can hear but not see
What rejuvenates but doesn't drain
Over the flock it floats
Float sweet spirit float
For too many here you are unknown
But on today you will be felt
Give site to the sightless
Give ears to the death
Give words to the mute
And to the breathless give breath
For they want to know of you
But are lacking in their understanding
Guide us oh hope of all hope
Let us delight in your spirit
Oh sweet Holy Ghost

THE JUNGLE

I sleep with the animals, every foul
beast of the field;

The prayers that fell upon the Lords

ears are the only reason I live.

That very same beast is my brother
barely breathing,

fighting the same struggle as I;

As they gasp I cry but only on the inside;

Because that tear would uncloak me and

they would know that I am man and not beast.

They would rip me for being
what they consider

false and on my carcass they would feast;

Ruthless are my brothers for the laws

of the field are all they know;

Teeth sharpened by the poison pored

from the glass bottle and the trees they blow.

Sickening the death that descends onto the

fields killing most beasts but some escape;

I am but one and yet and still I lay.

In the fields with the beast and still I cry;

Because I know they can only teach the cubs

what they have done to survive.

The prayers that shielded me I now
use to shield them;

Hoping the cycle will stop with them
through the love of him,

OUR FATHER.

Got To Know Life

Life is so very splendid when you
can see it in motion,
When you can see it run,
When you can see it walk,
When you can see it bouncing a ball and then
turning it into a game,
When you can see how beautiful it is,
When you can see it young and see it old,
When it's happy or when it's sad,
When you can see its joys and pains,
When you can hear the loving tones
both soft and loud,
When you can turn nothing into
something or someone,
When you can value it, young or old,
I say then you know life.

My Brothers

> Brothers, we are not God's gift to women.
>
> Women are God's gift to us……. let that marinate.

The Perfect Poem

The perfect poem, sung in a soul
with no pulse;
No heart beat… no emotion;
No fear of death because
for him dieing was not
just a notion, but a promise;
That promise only lacking a date and a time;
Ignorance not a barrier;
Just that very thin line;
Inside a cup;
That cup knowledge would
have him sip from but
not swallow;
But he does swallow;
He could never lead men because
he himself refuses to follow;
His heart hollowed,
From what the world has
forced him to swallow;
And he can't teach you much

because what he
knows he has barrowed from
a book unwritten;
That lye's deep in the bowels of hells kitchen;
As his lids roll back and eyes glisten
from the thoughts of escaping
his own prison;
But he can't rejoice the
fullest existents because
he is still missing that pulse,
that heart beat, that emotion;
That drive;
That thrill one feels from just being alive;
You see for him life
was the saddest reflection of death;
And he had written chapters on it for scores
only to be tossed aside;
So he doesn't write anything
before closing his
eyes, see the perfect poem
he was, but he died;

Committed suicide;
To live to breath to die;
Suicide of the perfect poem;
And all he wanted was to be heard.

I am here

That dark corner where people
are afraid to turn,
I stood at it and faced it all alone,
As a child I smiled and enjoyed
it because society
convinced me that's
where I belonged,
There in that dark place,
Where many before me had to face,
The man-child being erased from the
happiest saddest little face,
They said a child should stay
in a child's place,
But that's a place that this child
had never been,
For in an alley way standing
facing death drowning
in a world of sin,
is where I was,
Only reaching adulthood to be betrayed
by a heart I had never had,
Four walls closing in trying to crush
the path laid out for me,
See I crawled through the belly
of the beast that
I had long since left behind,
I fought a raging river that gave way to a
horrendous raging water wall
refusing to be denied,
But I stand here thanking God to be alive!

Mind your steps

Let them not accompany the faint
hearted or the unwilling,

For in your way lie hurdles, barriers
and a number of other obstacles that where
lay down by you…yourself,

There leaving so much clutter
for you to sift through,

Therefore you must mind your steps,

Mind and mend your way,

So that henceforth you can be
lead as well as lead,

Without stumbling in the wake of the clutter of
those who are unwilling to take that step,

Mind your steps,

And know that as long as your steps are
concentrated upon and you are not critical of
others steps,

Your steps will prosper,

For every day of your life,

Mind your steps,

Just a little more each and every second of every hour of every day,

Mind your steps and God will bless you,

For you are willing.

Burn

Though scared from the fire I don't

feel the burns,

Still amazed by the lesson in life I've

lived to learn,

If I have it please know that in this

life I've surely earned,

Money and power never a

real mans concerns,

Though I'm wealthy in more ways than

man's mind can fathom,

That man in the mirror I still find my self

running to catch him,

I have questions that only he or

God can answer,

For I've turned a lot of pages but I haven't

found any answers to so many questions,

Like why did so much have to happen to me,

As a baby I had all ready opened

my eyes to see,

That this day and time was not meant for me,

But a lot of places in it I was meant to be,

So was I suppose to be weaker than a man

that came before me,

Was all the weight on my back to show

that I was more than eyes could see?

Though scared from the fire I

don't feel the burns,

But I'll never forget them and the

lesson I've learned.

Soul of an Old Song

These young bones rest in the soul
of an old song
Sam Cook once sung,
A change is gonna come,
In an old Negro hymn sung by my
grandmother as she stewed fresh picked
greens over a wood burning stove,
Way up in the Georgia Mountains were
the green grass still grows,
Strong to its roots even in the snow,
In a log cabin surrounded by tall
fresh green pine,
Every single tree housing a spirit
as old as mine,
In an iceberg that has circled the artic twice,
Concealed in side of a kiss that
joins two lives,
In an old guitar with strings that hammer off
notes that have endured the years,
Inside the old woman's smile as
she sheds a tear,
That's where I am and where I belong,
Let my soul be forever trapped inside
of an old song.

One and the Same

Laminated practices birth from
forefathers whom
came before our forefathers

Continue to sway the masses into
this belief of one
man actually being greater than another

My brother and my brother's brother can't
seem to maneuver their way through a
shattered dialect that has held man
bond for centuries

The dismal language of the
rich disrupts the so
called minuscule language of the poor

Both cry the same cry
bleed the same blood
but yet they are considered
to be so vastly different

Ignorance follows the rich as well as the poor
None knowing a pinch more than
the other about life

The remains of the rich will be ash
as will the poor will be

If both focus on what's at hand they
both shall reach an end

One can make it to the middle
and one can stay
near the front but still both must
come to the end

Once it was said a rich man's trash
is a poor man's treasure

But at some point it must have been the rich
man's treasure because he himself
once possessed it

No different
one in the same they are and will forever be

Because we are only men
Despite rich or poor we are only men

I Can

If you want the moon baby I got that
for you this past May

Like money in a vault I have it locked
up and stored away

If you want the stars just for extra
I can gather them all today

And place roses on a few just to see
the smile on your face

A lake
that's nothing when I can give
you all seven sea's

Make it where you would be
the air that I breathe

If you want hills I'll give you mountains
you want roses I'll give you fields

You want romance
that I can give for as long as we live

You want paper
I'll leave now and start cutting down trees

To show you that you are worth
that much work to me

The heavens and the earth can be
yours all at the same time

Because that's what you deserve
when you are mine

I know it doesn't seem possible
when it comes from a simple man

But know that maybe others can't
but this man can

Know your fight

For they fought with Great Spirit
And they were as brave as they were scared
But their fight lasted not
For as the sun grew weak
And the moon grew strong
Their will to continue grew faint
Their cause was loosing its cause
As well as its momentum
Engulfed in an uncontrollable commotion
Delusions of a piece of peace
Come over them all
Assuring in many of their minds
That the fight that they where so passionately
Fighting was not worth fighting at all

They Win

Four walls couldn't hold me,

So they tried bars and chains,

They tried shackles, ropes and barbed wire,
and still I came,

To this point where freedom flows through my
veins like the waters in the rushing river,

But still I speak not,
when I should stand and deliver,

But let them take my voice, my whisper,
and even my cries,

Let them take my view or the sight from both
my eyes,

My hands, both my arms, and even my legs
and both my thighs,

Then at that moment I'll say in a voice I've
never heard,

They win and I had my chance….

Mercy Mercy

As the moon births bright rays
of illuminating color

The hands of passion steady a
pen in the corner
of a poorly lit room

His hands resilient
steadied by the task at hand

Giving no thought to the narrow-minded\
views of those
who will curse his lyric

He melts slowly down into a chair that
he has committed him self to

With a distilled taste in his mouth
and he and his emotions in full agreement
this piece will be as close to flawless
as mans ears had ever heard

This lyric will serve as a testament to all those
who have endured disorder and corruption

It shall not be vulgar so that
one generation of seeds after another
may retrieve its wealth of honesty

It will serve as retribution to
all those whom had no voice
To those who have suffered for
the sake of suffering

It will sum up the animated docile creature
that lives and breathes death in his
home-land

It will not be the rhetoric of a fool
but of the scarred

It will be absolute
leaving an indefinite mark
on all its shadow is cast upon

With his eye-lids soaked he writes
Mercy, mercy me
Brother Marvin
you were heard
and you where felt

It wasn't

Night falls and that inescapable feeling of
being held captive by the spoils of something
that wasn't

For that time was none existent
But I insisted that it was when it wasn't

The false love in me escapes through the
gates of my soul

Those gates left open by the lies that fled
through them

The weight of what festers and the presents
of all that lie dormant and bare start to restrict
my blood flow

So I lay suffocating
gasping for a breath that isn't
that never was
that wasn't

My dilution of so called love
was no more than an addiction

An addiction to something that I forced
myself to believe was
When it wasn't
it just wasn't…

Discontent

I am discontent with this world

Discontent with this life

Discontent with what is wrong

Discontent with what is right

Discontent wit the unlawful

Discontent with the law abiding

Discontent with this government

And a president that is always lying

I am discontent with cats having nine lives

Discontent with working a nine to five

Discontent with stretching ends to buy a ride

And working a side job just to get by

I am discontent with people who are

self-righteous

Discontent with the self-loafing

I am discontent with the depressed and those whom fear growing

I am discontent with the brave

I am discontent with the weak

Discontent with those who change their voice whenever they are around mix-company

I am discontent with being discontent

I am discontent for so many reasons

I'll be discontent tomorrow

Because I am a discontent….being

I am discontent with those whom are critical

Discontent with the meek

Well……I can face the fact that

I am most of all

Discontent with me……….

Hello Day Break

Hello day break
So we meet again

And again I stand before you naked as you
always come before me so that we may
examine each other you and I

You and I are so similar day break
for you shine light onto the world
and my mission in life is to
shed light onto the world

You and I are so similar day break
you and I both peak over the horizon before
coming out completely

You and I both do what we must
to fight off the dark clouds

We both live in the sky so blue

because so many swear I share
that space with you

They say my head stays in the clouds
but I say I am like you day break
I just enjoy shining

I enjoy it not being a day unless I'm in it
I enjoy being greater than I am viewed

You see day-break we seem so meaningless
but we shine so much light

Day-break I am your brother in the south
just saying hello
day break…

Tomorrows Death

If one tenth of the soul could love
any and all things,
just how would a life of living be?
How or what would the gentle eyes of a
child spawn out of love see,
Life is an understanding that is easily
misrepresented
and misunderstood,
So that love that is life is the same,
Misunderstood…
Viewed more as a bad thing rather than good,
We stand at the forefront of something that
was not designed to be carried
in a mans heart,
But we do carry it,
A hate for love and it's sad
that this is
tearing us apart,
Men and women would rather have a
so-called friend than a soul mate,
We've cursed our children to quickly become
subdued and fall into this same state,
To much corruption to be erased,
We've developed a fear and a
hatred for commitment
both developed at the same instants,
So a tomorrow of love is becoming
so very non-existent,
Non-existent… This is tomorrow's death….

Refuge

Sometime ago my feelings ran from me
seeking refuge from the dark
waves of surrender,
Only to find that those waves were bound to
me for reasons unexplained
as well as unknown,
But as I sift through the ruble I find a gem,
That gem and I are one in the same,
That gem so very precious for that gem has
endured those same dark waves as I,
She too sought refuge in a heart from a heart
only to find that a home for her heart was
miles away from the home she
had grown to know,
She followed the crooked waterway to find
what was thought to be copper,
But in fact was truly gold,
She found a home for her heart in a heart that
desired her heart as well as called out to her,
No longer seek refuge,
My gem you are home,
Home in my heart…

Changing Spots

Life is too short for me to be trying to be too many people at one time,

It is hard enough being me,

And being me suits me just fine,

I am confident I can captain this ship if my crew would just follow my lead,

As long as they respect themselves as well as respect me,

Me personally, I can't handle transition so I don't just up and change my spots all that often,

Many that I know make that mistake and either get caught up or lost in,

A place in a moment with some one they never knew,

But the strangest thing is you change your spots so often that you never knew that stranger was you.

Here

Stand here…
Stand here where the four corners of the
earth all meet at one point,
Stand here where the boiling point is
lower than the freezing point,
Stand here where a man's
heartbeat is greater
than the booms of a billion cannons,
Stand here where sensitivity is not
considered a sign of weakness,
Stand here where the belief
in God is still evident,
Stand here where a fathers' love for his
children can make the earth tremble,
Stand here where the power of a word can
still build and shape,
Stand here where a man still feels a woman
is to be appreciated and not degraded,
Stand here where smiles
are better than frowns,
were love is greater than hate,
Where opening the door or pulling up a
woman's chair is still considered noble,
Stand here my brother and
you can stand with me.

Wake me please

I beat on the walls as I wrestle with pimps
prostitutes and bare-foot blind beast

I see two bald demons kneeling near a small
thrown placed at the back heal of my feet

While muggers
and drunk drivers
continue to haunt me

Chasing me from point A
all the way back to point B
I'm running…

The person chasing me
resembles me from head to toe

So I stop to confront myself
but noticed not where I go

Confused
heart beating faster
but my blood starts to slow

As I collapse onto the pavement
A preacher stands over me asking
were the saved went
I jump up breathing hard
trying my best to make sense

Of this world full of deceit
horror and a whole lot of nonsense

Only to find that the third realm leaves me
thoroughly unconscious

So I beg bowed at the legs of a giant
as tall as a mountain

Asking is he God
as a six hundred pound she beast taps
on my shoulder offering sex and lies

As eye turn to look up at her
I noticed that she has no eyes

So I start to call on Jesus to save
me from all these hideous things

Then I wake to find there is power in his
name…

XXXXXXXX

Judge me not if you know not my tragedies,
But for those who do, pity not me,
For I was born son of a man,
A man who never could stand,
In this arena in which I now stand,
Yet what ever I've done came from
the heart of a man,
A woman bore me out of pain, guilt and debt,
Through torment she gave birth to the son
she has never met,
I could sit and tell her of my heart aches but
she would never know,
That the demons that chased her
chase her son also,
For I was stoned for being right,
And for my wrongs I was stoned twice,
I fought to move forward in this life,
A life where I'm persecuted for believing that
God carries the shield which protects me.

Find your way

It appears peaceful to the right of me but the clouds grow darker by the hour,

And before long darkness has fallen upon the entire area so quickly it devours everything,

> Everything in that sector
> nothing casting shadow,

> Alleyways give way to
> screeches and screams,

> Beat back by the afflictions that
> deadened my dreams,

An echo in the air carries through the darkness as the wind taps on my shoulder,

> My legs bent as I cry singing
> a song to Jehovah,

> Darkened but not black is my heart
> and my soul as well,

Raging war inside of me some spirit from hell,
It tells me that I will surly die,

> But that battle is not mine its God's.

4x4

I need a witness…
Do I have a witness…
Oh I need a witness…
A witness to tatter tears…
15 years…
And 2 months on a forty man tier…
Consecutive years…
Of sights unseen…
Eyes sown shut as freedom rings…
As the blood flows slowly down
a concrete ravine…
I need a witness…
A witness to men scared by other men…
Brothers getting sliced from their
stomachs to their chins…
Your greatest enemy is your closest friend…
I cannot hold back what lies within,
No matter what is said
I feel as though I am doomed,
Trapped here in this 4x4 cold solitary room.

(Live What) My Life or Yours

Live they said, so we of course did just that,
Not live just but just live,
Not live and let live but just live,
Not live and learn but just live,
Not live with minimal concern but just live,
Not be responsible and live but just live,
Not care for your fellow man but just live,
Not recognize your wrongs but just live,
Not be honest but just live,
Not have love for others but just live,
Not wonder about God's plan but just live,
Not want to understand but just live,
Do not want peace for all man kind just live,
Not want what is rightfully yours but just live,
I ask you my friend live what!!!
My life!
Or yours!

You can not define me

You cannot define me by a color
You cannot define me
by my brother

You cannot define me by my once
alcohol and drug addicted mother

Cannot define me by my sister
Cannot define me by my dad
No you can't define me by the
troubled times in life I once had

Can't define me by the
clothes I like to wear

Cannot define me by how I like
to keep my hair

Can't define me by how I use to
live when you were never there

You cannot define how strong I am
Cannot determine if I am weak
You cannot determine how smart I am by
simply hearing me speak

Cannot determine if I am a coward
Cannot determine if I am just brave

Cannot determine if I just love the world
or if I just love being saved

You cannot define my anger
Cannot define how much I am
meant to be

Cannot determine just how much my spiritual
eyes will allow me to see

You cannot determine if I am here to mislead
or if I am here to truthfully teach

There is one thing you can define and that is
the fact that you cannot define me

So instead of trying to determine what defines
me here is what you should do

Though it may seem hard at first
try to determine what defines you

Because you cannot define me
oh no you cannot define me

Page 3 my diary

Deploy my heart I will to you,
Dispatching all the love I
have ever known,
For seas have wept forbiddingly
do to my sorrow,
That sorrow has fitted my soul with a surreal
burning shackle,
That shackle symbolizing and inkling of the
time we have spent apart,
For this moment you are not near me starts to
deaden my pulse,
And I am becoming faint,
My heart beat is slowly diminishing,
As I cry out love,
Love where are you?
Do you not hear my cries?
Do you not sense the urgency in my voice?
I stand still in a house with no
doors or windows,
Hoping you will find your way back in,
Love come to me,
My cries, now screams,
are becoming hard blows to parts
of my person
few ever knew existed,
I drop to my knees and with my faded,
weakening voice I cry out one last time,
Love where are you, do you not hear me?
Page 3 of my diary.

You owe

I can only live my life because
I owe it to myself,

I can only be who I am, as I am, because I
owe this to myself,

I must love you as I love me because I owe
this to myself,

I must stand for what I believe because I owe
this to myself,

I must always fight the good fight because I
owe this to myself,

I can not fight your battles,
I have my own; I owe that to myself,

In this world, know that know one owes you
anything, most things you just owe yourself,

So learn to love and understand yourself
before your days come to an end, make
peace with yourself and you will make peace
with all,

You owe it to yourself!

Brick yard

Stares are frost bitten
and distant
in the brickyard

Mourners
Killers
Cutthroats
and thieves
are found
in the brickyard

Seldom is anything ever left to discard
Everything is everything
in the brickyard

Horror movies have nothing
on the brickyard

Abandoned boxes and cars
are shelter
in the brickyard

Alleys and hallways
are death traps
in the brickyard

The only help you have
is God
in the brickyard

Fallen mommas
are guardian angels
in the brickyard

If you get caught up
you better know
no one over here saw it

That's just one of the codes
of the brickyard

A fight always draws blood
in the brickyard

Seldom is anything truth
in the brickyard

Dreams are not lived
but crushed
by the brickyard

Thousands are lost every day
to the brickyard

Many don't understand the ways
of the brickyard

Crippled by lack we are
in the brickyard

Some run and can't turn back
from the brickyard

Many have sold their souls
to the brickyard

No one fears or knows of the devil
in the brickyard

You want to battle the beast
come to the brickyard

We are born without peace
in the brickyard

How come I know so much
about the brickyard?

I'm one of the drug-dealing thieves born
to the streets of the brickyard.

Keep Walking

If I walk half way with you just
how far will you go?

I am just a man
so it is only fair that you know,
that half way is all I can offer,
and I cannot truly offer that.

I am compelled to ask you this,
because I want to know,
if you will look back.

Will you watch me
as I walk on to continue my journey?

Or will you just wonder on
that same little patch of road?

Or will you continue on
watching your steps to see
what will unfold?

Will you focus on the task at hand or will you
just stop where you are?

I cannot continue to hold your hand friend
because I can only go so far.

You must not focus on me for I
am only a man like you.
Keep your eyes on the road and let
God lead you through.

I've got a man

Breathe my sister
for he cannot suffocate you
in such a manner that demoralizes
your very state of being

For you are
a creature of God
his eyes most be clouded
because he is not seeing

The beauty he has
in a sister such as your self

Forgive me my sister
but I must ask

Is this man in good health?

Not physically
but mentally

Is he right within his spirit?

See it is not you he hates
it is the God in you he fears
and he is not willing to hear this

You tell him right
he says you are wrong

so quite naturally you reply
You may say what you want my dear but
my father does not lie

Your cup is flowing over
because of what God has put
inside of you

So he refrains from speaking much
longer because he sees God taking over
and he fears that very truth of the light
because he loves the night the darkness

It is so powerfully sweet to his nature
this is why it seems as if this brother hates
you

***But you continue to love
until God says stop!***

Until then stay and hold your ground

If he says he leaving
fear not my sister
you have a real man around

As you said before
you can say once more
Your father does not lie

You have a man!

Values

Family values seem to escape through
the sin filled pores of the retched

As their minds start to decay from the
over dose of what the world truly expected

Them to become subjected to when they
entered out in to these diseased
infested lands

Pestilence fills the hourglass forever
replacing the sands

Of time as it draws near it is evident that
the last days draw even closer

I pray on the Day of Judgment we were
taught enough to get us over

Those things we have entombed in side
ourselves since our very beginning

Entrusting in immoral teachings
what will be our ending

On the street corners we teach our sons
pimping fast cars dice games and dope

We educate our daughters on how to work a
failing welfare system so they
quickly loose hope

These sons and daughters go and pop out
babies as early as 12 and 13 years old

These sons flee from what they were never
shown and what they really refuse to know

To hold my daughter and son in my arms on
the
day they were born

Set off an alarm

I must break the curses that have
fallen upon me

And do what I know I can do

I must not do as my father or my
father's father

I must have family values

Alone

Cold blows to the soul left a hole
where my heart was;

Being real to a feeling many a
man has been a victim of;

Falling into a shell that does not crack, but
hardens every time the wind blows fond
memories of yesterday;

The dawn comes the morning dew passes
over my limp body as I lay;

Still in the yard of the guilty,
the scorn and the mistrusted;

Blinded by a inner man that has
lied cheated and lusted;

For something that never came to be
upon a righteous mans surface;

Never would I believe another
person could have birthed this;

Hatred for something I once enjoyed so
much but now that's gone;

I use to enjoy the quiet time,
but now I hate to being alone;

But I am alone.

What good is a poem

What good is a poem?
What good is a poem?
What good is a poem?

What good is a poem if it
cannot move or grip?

A poem should flow smoothly from a poets
tongue and simply fall from masterful lips.

What good is a poem if it cannot
sway the masses?

Giving them thoughts of love
peace and happiness.

What good is a poem?

What good is a poem if it is only about pain,
torment, torture and the misery train?

What good is a poem?

What good is a poem if not viewed in more
than just plain black and white.

What good is a poem that is not in color if it
cannot shed light?

What good is a poem?

What good is a poem that does
not exist in love?

What good is a poem if it is not all that you
have ever dreamed of?

What good is a poem if it cannot take you
from then to now, from adult to child, if it
cannot make you smile?

What good is a poem?

What good is a poem if you cannot
live that poem?
Cannot give that poem,
Cannot breath that poem,

You see that poem should be undying,
That poem should be defining,
It should bind together what people thought to
be unbinding,

Unbinding that poem,
You should respect that poem,
Never disrespect that poem,
Protect that poem never
suppress that poem,

Digest that poem,
Beat in your chest that poem,

You should listen to that poem heed
the voice of that poem,

That poem should be you as well as I,
That poem should summons our emotions
and dry our eyes if we should cry,

That poem for me is my father
that is in heaven,
My family that consists of seven,
That poem is my beautiful wife,
That poem is my life,

For that poem I give thanks to God,
I am standing with my poem.

My giant

Who drinks of the crystal river to
quench their thirst?

Has a heart that beats so loudly
that it shakes the earth.

A giant does.

What has a mammoth appetite for
life and all of its intangibles?

Can lift and move mountains and jump so
high it appears they are flying?

A giant does.

What can reach all the things you are short of
and make the big things around you appear
so small?

A giant does.

What lifts the world on its shoulders
without strain?

A modern day marvel that's as
sweet as the sky is blue,

A giant is.

I have met a giant and you may think that what I say is not true.

But believe me when I say I have met a giant.

Not only that, I married that giant.

My wife is my giant.

She is as strong as a thousand men,

As gentle as a butterfly,

As tall as the tree lines,

And she pulls down the stars just for me,

She is my hero and my giant.

War inside me

It's almost like I am trapped
but not stuck
confined to a place
I never asked to be

Searching a field
I never asked to come to
nor did I ask to see

Could this be what hell is like?

And if so
does it burn like this fire
in this place I never ask to come to?

I mean is it filled with the grunge and smoke
so thick that you can't muster a view to see
through?

The Rules Are

The rules of life seem to be a little
misleading don't they?

The way they shift
the way they fold,

The ultimate poker hand so you
can only play the hand you hold,

I used to like this game of life
and the way it was played,

But the rules in this game
are to few I must say.

We all get to choose which part
of the game in life we wish to play,

The part of the game I now choose works
better for me for the rules have all ready
been set,

It has been around as long as man
and I know what to expect,

The rules are all written
and the refs' always watching
never making a bad call in the game,

Now the other part of life's game

is quite different
the rules are always subject to change,

It is hard to maintain when the
rules always change,

Sunshine, sleet, or snow you even
continue in the rain,

This game never stops no one will come
and relieve you for a break,

For me though when I get tired I just
call on my coach and teammate,

That guy that deceived you isn't on your
team he's playing the same game as you,

It is you against the world
no matter what you do,

You want a little help
I'll tell you what you can do,

Come join this more honest game, because
as you can see your game has but one rule,

That rule seems to keep you quite confused,

But that rule is very clear to me for in that
part there are no rules.

Pick it Up

One day a man was walking through the park when he met up with another brother whom he noticed was going through some things.

He approached him and asked what was wrong. The brother began to tell him about all that he had been through. The man understood his pain because he to remembered how it was when he was in the world. He then began to tell the brother about the light and the glory of God.

The brother said, "I don't understand." The man said, "come to the sidewalk and we'll show you." As they walked over to the sidewalk the man picked up five sticks in one had and a fist full of sand in the other.

When they made it to the sidewalk the man said, "Can you count the sticks in my hand?"

The brother responded "why yes." As he said it the man dropped the sticks to the surface of the sidewalk and said, "pick them up."

As the brother retrieved them the man said, "in your hands how many sticks do you hold?" The brother said, "the five you dropped." The man said, "yes, and they landed on the walkway where you could clearly see them all."

You were able to see exactly how many were dropped and where I dropped them." The brother responded, "yes of course." The man said, "now step off the sidewalk back to the surface of the world with the grass and the dirt."

He then asked "can you see the sand in my hand"? "Why yes", said the brother. As he responded the man dropped the sand to the ground and said "pick it up."

The brother looked shocked and stunned and said "how can I pick up the grains of sand when I know not where they fall?" The man said, you know not where because you have let so many mount your blind shoulders so they are too small and too many for you to see and manage.

When you come into the light of God you are blinded no longer. You can see your problems, your faults, and you now have someone to help you overcome any obstacle you are faced with.

The light guides us all my brother, come out of the world so that you may see as clearly as this. For my God is masterful in all things and to have you with him is his greatest gift, and in return his gift to you is everlasting light."

Peace

A lot of people these days tend to forget where they're from

I beat on my chest to make the rhythm of the drums

And I watch my people come

See I was born in the slums

So by ignorance I was stung

I drink poison by a tree in which my forefathers were hung

Yet they say to me man act your color

So to those I say I do my brother

by trying to teach the others who don't know their mothers

And don't know their fathers

Those who didn't' know that the author of pain was a scholar

Shifty eyed and blue colored

who cared nothing about color

Only nickels
Dimes
credit cards and benefits

And anything else that
can make some sense

I teach and you turn
a blind eye and a death ear to me.

You dismiss the disciple
of uplifting the streets

You see soldier are
not a dime a dozen to me

So you can just leave me be

Cause the revolution for me

Now is clearly about peace

www.ingramcontent.com/pod-product-compliance
Ingram Content Group UK Ltd.
Pitfield, Milton Keynes, MK11 3LW, UK
UKHW022208230426
12048UKWH00016BA/722